My First Pet

Hermit Crabs

by Vanessa Black

Bullfrog Books

Ideas for Parents and Teachers

Bullfrog Books let children practice reading informational text at the earliest reading levels. Repetition, familiar words, and photo labels support early readers.

Before Reading

- Discuss the cover photo. What does it tell them?

- Look at the picture glossary together. Read and discuss the words.

Read the Book

- "Walk" through the book and look at the photos. Let the child ask questions. Point out the photo labels.

- Read the book to the child, or have him or her read independently.

After Reading

- Prompt the child to think more. Ask: What do you need to take care of a hermit crab? Would you like one as a pet?

Bullfrog Books are published by Jump!
5357 Penn Avenue South
Minneapolis, MN 55419
www.jumplibrary.com

Library of Congress Cataloging-in-Publication Data

Names: Black, Vanessa, author.
Title: Hermit crabs / by Vanessa Black.
Description: Minneapolis, MN: Jump!, Inc., [2017]
Series: My first pet | Audience: Age 5–8.
Audience: K to grade 3. | Includes index.
Identifiers: LCCN 2016026923 (print)
LCCN 2016027196 (ebook).
ISBN 9781620315521 (hardcover: alk. paper)
ISBN 9781624965005 (ebook)
Subjects: LCSH: Hermit crabs as pets—
Juvenile literature.
Classification: LCC SF459.H47 B57 2017 (print)
LCC SF459.H47 (ebook) | DDC 639/.67—dc23
LC record available at https://lccn.loc.gov/2016026923

Editor: Kirsten Chang
Book Designer: Michelle Sonnek
Photo Researcher: Michelle Sonnek

Photo Credits: All photos by Shutterstock except: Alamy, cover, 1, 20–21; Craig Cook, 14–15; Dwight Kuhn, 17; Getty, 3; iStock, 13, 18–19, 22, 23br, 24; Thinkstock, 6–7.

Printed in the United States of America at Corporate Graphics in North Mankato, Minnesota.

Table of Contents

A Class Pet

We want a pet
for our class.

Ms. Sun is our teacher.
She loves sea animals.
What should she get us?

5

Hermit crabs!
We will help
care for them.

Ms. Sun gets
a big glass tank.

It has a lid.

Li puts in sand.

She adds fake plants.

She adds rocks.

Pat turns on a heat lamp.
It keeps the crabs warm.

Jo sprays water in the tank.
Crabs need humid air.

water
dish

Len adds a water dish.
The crabs crawl in
to drink.

May puts in food.
She adds kale.

She adds fish.
She adds fruit.

17

Uma adds
empty shells.

As crabs grow,
they need
bigger shells.

shells

Crabs make cool pets!

What Does a Hermit Crab Need?

glass tank
Get a tank that is at least 10 gallons (38 liters). For more crabs, choose a larger tank.

heat lamp
Use a heat lamp to keep your hermit crab's home above 75 degrees Fahrenheit (24 degrees Celsius).

accessories
Provide rocks or fake plants for your crabs to climb on, but not real plants. Crabs could eat them and get sick.

shells
Offer your crab a variety of shapes and sizes. Do not include painted shells; they can harm your crab.

water
Provide one dish of fresh water and one dish of salt water.

Picture Glossary

fake
Not real.

kale
A leafy green vegetable.

humid
Having a high water content.

shells
Hard, protective coverings.

Index

To Learn More

Learning more is as easy as 1, 2, 3.

1) Go to www.factsurfer.com

2) Enter "pethermitcrabs" into the search box.

3) Click the "Surf" button to see a list of websites.

With factsurfer.com, finding more information is just a click away.